D0917410

SCIENCE HIGHLIGHTS

1900–1946

THE AGE OF THE ATOM

By Charlie Samuels

Gareth Stevens
Publishing

Please visit our Web site www.garethstevens.com. For a free color catalog of all our high-quality books, call toll free 1-800-542-2595 or fax 1-877-542-2596.

Library of Congress Cataloging-in-Publication Data
Samuels, Charlie, 1961-
  The age of the atom (1900-1946) / Charlie Samuels.
    p. cm. — (Science highlights)
  Includes index.
  ISBN 978-1-4339-4151-1 (lib. bdg.)
  ISBN 978-1-4339-4152-8 (pbk.)
  ISBN 978-1-4339-4153-5 (6-pack)
  1. Inventions—History—20th century—Juvenile literature. 2. Discoveries in science—History--20th century—Juvenile literature. I. Title.
  Q180.55.D57S26 2011
  609.'041—dc22

                              2010015047

Published in 2011 by
Gareth Stevens Publishing
111 East 14th Street, Suite 349
New York, NY 10003

© 2010 The Brown Reference Group Ltd.

For Gareth Stevens Publishing:
Art Direction: Haley Harasymiw
Editorial Direction: Kerri O'Donnell

For The Brown Reference Group Ltd:
Editorial Director: Lindsey Lowe
Managing Editor: Tim Cooke
Editor: Ben Hollingum
Children's Publisher: Anne O'Daly
Design Manager: David Poole
Designer: Kim Browne
Picture Manager: Sophie Mortimer
Production Director: Alastair Gourlay

Picture Credits:
Front Cover: Shutterstock

Inside: Corbis: Doug Wilson 31; **iStockphoto:** 14; **NASA:** GRIN 5, 26, 29; Apollo Gallery 22, 23, 24; **Public Domain:** Museum of Science, Boston 9; **Science Photo Library:** Corning Inc/Emilio Segre Visual Archives/American Institute of Physics 15; **Shutterstock:** Andrew Bazylchik 18; Ferenc Cegledi 42; R Fonzales 30; Galaxy Photo 33(t); Maram 44; Catalan Petolea 45; Richard Waters 39; **Thinkstock:** Brand X Pictures 7(t); comstock 10, 17; istockphoto 8, 11, 13, 16, 33(b), 35, 41; Hemera 19, 38; Photos.com 6, 7(b); Valueline 21; **Topfoto:** 37; PA 34;

All Artworks The Brown Reference Group

The Brown Reference Group has made every attempt to contact copyright holders. If anyone has any information please contact info@brownreference.com

Manufactured in the United States of America
1 2 3 4 5 6 7 8 9 12 11 10

CPSIA compliance information: Batch #CS10GS: For further information contact Gareth Stevens, New York, New York at 1-800-542-2595.

Contents

Introduction 4

The Invention of Radio 6

The First Automobiles 10

The Airplane 14

Synthetic Drugs 18

Subatomic Particles 22

The First Television 26

Penicillin and Antibiotics 30

The Development of Radar 34

Wernher von Braun 38

Nuclear Fission 42

Glossary 46

Further Reading 47

Index 48

Introduction

The first half of the 20th century was dominated by two world wars. As always, conflict encouraged technological development as combatants raced to get an advantage.

The most promising area of scientific exploration was the nature of atoms, the particles that made them up, and the power they contained. Nowhere did increased knowledge of the atomic and subatomic world have more profound effects than in electronics. The work of theoretical physicists such as Albert Einstein, who sought to understand the very nature of the universe itself, led to a practical appreciation of radio waves and the development of radio and TV. In transportation, meanwhile, the coming of the airplane and the automobile were to be equally revolutionary. Not for the first time in history, scientific advances were changing the ways people communicated—and even how they thought.

The Influence of Warfare

In the shadow of the two world wars (1914–1918 and 1939–1945), weaponry became more powerful; an understanding of radio waves led to the technology of radar. Medical care advanced, too, with the creation of the first antibiotic, penicillin.

In the early 1940s, scientists in Britain and the United States experimented with unlocking the power of the atom. Just three years after they created the first controlled nuclear chain reaction in a room in Chicago, the atom bombs were dropped on Japan.

About This Book

This book uses timelines to describe scientific and technological advances from about 1900 to about 1950. A continuous timeline of the period runs along the bottom of all the pages. Its entries are color-coded to indicate the different fields of science to which they belong. Each chapter also has its own subject timeline, which runs vertically down the edge of the page.

Radio spread rapidly through the 1920s and 1930s as a means of mass communication. It gave people increased access to everything from sports to politics. ↓

The Invention of Radio

Radio uses electromagnetic radiation, known as radio waves, which travel at the speed of light. It was called "wireless" to distinguish it from telegraphs and telephones.

← Radios became common in many homes in the United States and Europe in the 1920s.

TIMELINE
1900–1902

KEY:

Astronomy and Math

Biology and Medicine

Chemistry and Physics

Engineering and Invention

1900 Austrian neurologist Sigmund Freud publishes his seminal book *The Interpretation of Dreams*.

1900 Cuban-born U.S. physiologist Aristides Agramonte y Simoni discovers that yellow fever is transmitted through the bite of a mosquito.

1901 Japanese-born U.S. chemist Jokichi Takamine isolates epinephrine (adrenaline).

1900

1901

1900 German physicist Max Planck proposes the quantum theory: that radiation is emitted in separate "packets," or quanta.

1900 The rigid airship LZ-1, designed by German engineer Graf Ferdinand von Zeppelin, makes its first flight.

1900 U.S. inventor Thomas Edison invents the nickel–iron accumulator (Ni-Fe cell).

Timeline

1864 Radio waves predicted

1887 Discovery of radio waves

1890 Coherer for detecting radio waves

1894 Marconi's first radio transmissions

1903 Amplitude modulation (AM)

1904 Diode vacuum tube

1906 Triode vacuum tube

1933 Frequency modulation (FM)

Radio dates from the late 19th century. Scottish physicist James Clerk Maxwell predicted mathematically the existence of electromagnetic radiation in 1864. He decided that light is just one part of the spectrum of electromagnetic radiation. In 1887, German physicist Heinrich Hertz discovered a new type of radiation: radio waves.

Using Radio Waves

In 1890, French physicist Édouard Branly devised the first way of detecting radio waves using a "coherer," a sealed glass tube containing iron filings and an electrode at each end. When radio waves are present, the filings stick together and conduct electricity to form part of a circuit. English physicist Oliver Lodge improved it in 1894 and used it together with a spark transmitter to send Morse code messages a distance of 490 feet (150 m). Russian physicist Aleksandr Popov conducted similar experiments a year later.

Unaware of these developments, Italian physicist Guglielmo Marconi also began experimenting with radio in 1894. In the process, he invented a radio antenna and the use of a ground (earth) with the apparatus. He could soon transmit coded messages more than 1.8 miles (3 km). The invention, known as radiotelegraphy, developed rapidly, especially after Marconi moved to

↑ Some of the earliest radio transmissions used Morse code signals.

1901 English inventor Hubert Booth invents a vacuum cleaner powered by a gasoline engine.

1901 German physicist Karl Ferdinand Braun invents the crystal detector for tuning a radio.

1902 French surgeon Alexis Carrel develops a technique for joining blood vessels end to end with fine stitches (sutures).

1902

1901 Italian physicist Guglielmo Marconi makes the first transatlantic radio transmission.

1902 French meteorologist Léon Teisserenc de Bort distinguishes the stratosphere and troposphere layers in Earth's atmosphere.

1902 German chemist Emil Fischer determines that proteins are polypeptides, made up from chains of amino acids.

Amplitude Modulation

Radiotelephony relies on modulation: altering a constant signal by a varying one. An audio-frequency signal from a microphone is amplified to vary an oscillator's radio-frequency signal, which is reamplified then transmitted. At the receiver, an antenna picks up the transmitted signal. It is amplified before being demodulated and amplified to reproduce the original audio signal in a loudspeaker.

⟶ Either the strength or frequency of the constant carrier wave can be modulated.

England in 1896. By 1901, he could transmit signals in Morse code across the Atlantic Ocean.

So far radio was an improvement on the telegraph because it did not need wires to transmit signals. But could radio be made to carry human voices, like the telephone? This question led to the development of radiotelephony, when Canadian-born U.S. electrical engineer Reginald Fessenden invented modulation. Radiotelegraphy sends out pulses of short and long signals (the dots and dashes of Morse code). In radiotelephony, the transmitter sends out a continuous signal, a carrier wave, whose amplitude (strength) is varied (modulated) in step with the variations in the sound signals from a microphone. It allows the transmission of a range of sounds. Fessenden first demonstrated amplitude modulation (AM) in 1903. By 1906, he was able to transmit speech and music from a radio station in Massachusetts.

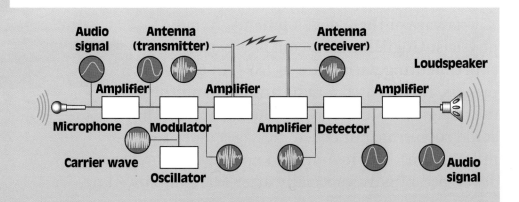

TIMELINE
1903–1904

1903 U.S. brothers Orville and Wilbur Wright make the first sustained flight in a heavier-than-air airplane.

1903 German surgeon Georg Perthes first uses X-rays to treat cancerous tumors.

1903 Russian astrophysicist Konstantin Tsiolkovsky proposes the first practical theory of rocket propulsion.

KEY:

1903

Astronomy and Math

Biology and Medicine

Chemistry and Physics

Engineering and Invention

1903 Dutch physiologist Willem Einthoven invents the electrocardiograph for recording electrical activity in the heart.

1903 Russian physiologist Ivan Pavlov develops the concept of the conditioned reflex (the way in which an action can be influenced by previous repetitive behavior).

Improved Detectors

The new system needed a better detector. It came in the form of an improved crystal detector. The detector connected to the radio circuit by an adjustable thin wire, which soon earned it the nickname "cat's whisker." In 1917, Marconi began making VHF (very high frequency) transmissions. By 1924, Marconi was also sending speech signals from England to Australia using shortwave radio.

Radio receivers improved in 1912 when Fessenden devised the heterodyne circuit, which allowed more selective tuning. In 1933, American engineer Edwin Armstrong invented FM (frequency modulation). In this technique, the frequency (not the amplitude) of the transmitted carrier wave is modulated by the broadcast signal. As a result, transmission was less sensitive to static, producing an increase in the quality of the received sound.

↓ Marconi built a radio station in Ireland to transmit signals across the Atlantic.

↑ Italian Guglielmo Marconi developed radio into a reliable means of international communications.

1904 English physicist J.J. Thompson puts forward his model of the atom: a spherical mass of positively charged matter with electrons embedded in it.

1904 English engineer John Fleming invents the diode valve (vacuum tube).

1904

1904 German astrophysicist Johannes Hartmann reveals the presence of interstellar matter in space.

1904 The first section of the New York City subway opens, with electric trains serving 28 stations.

1904 English chemist Arthur Harden discovers coenzymes, molecules that are needed to trigger the action of enzymes.

The First Automobiles

The automobile was the end result of a long effort to invent a motorized road vehicle. Early machines used a steam engine, the only motive power then available.

⟨⟨ A father and son show off their Model T Ford in the United States in the 1920s.

TIMELINE
1905–1907

KEY:

- Astronomy and Math
- Biology and Medicine
- Chemistry and Physics
- Engineering and Invention

1905 German-born U.S. physicist Albert Einstein publishes his special theory of relativity, one of the most important contributions in the history of science.

1905 French physicist Paul Langevin applies the electron theory to magnetic phenomena.

1906 French mathematician Maurice Fréchet introduces functional calculus.

1905

1906

1905 French psychologists devise a method of testing intelligence and ascribing an intelligence quotient (IQ).

1905 U.S. engineer Almon Strowger perfects the dial telephone.

1906 English geologist Richard Oldham deduces that Earth's core is molten.

In 1770, French engineer Nicolas-Joseph Cugnot built a three-wheel gun carriage, powered by a two-cylinder steam engine. Traveling at 3 miles (5 km) per hour, it had the world's first motor accident when it demolished a wall. German engineer Charles Dietz built another three-wheel machine in 1835. It used a pair of rocking cylinders that moved a chain drive to the rear wheels.

Experiments with steam vehicles continued to produce a tractor or multipassenger carriage rather than a personal vehicle. In England, William Murdock ran a

Timeline

1770 Cugnot's second steam-powered gun carriage

1829 Steam-powered road vehicle

1865 Lightweight steam carriage

1885 Benz three-wheeler

1886 Daimler four-wheel car

1893 Benz four-wheel car

1896 First U.S. automobile (Duryea) on sale

1908 Model T Ford

◄◄ The very first cars had only three wheels, but engineers soon favored the stability of four wheels. By the time of the Model T, tiller steering had been replaced by a steering wheel.

The first Benz car 1885

Panhard and Levassor 1894

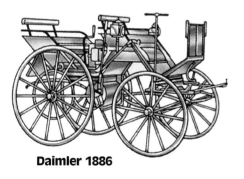

Daimler 1886

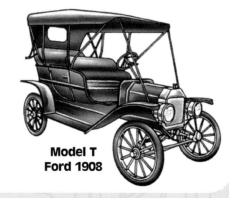

Model T Ford 1908

1906 New-Zealand born physicist Ernest Rutherford deduces that alpha particles (produced by radium emission) are helium nuclei.

1907 Belgian-born U.S. chemist Leo Baekeland invents Bakelite plastic.

1907 Swiss chemist Jacques Brandenburger prepares cellophane.

1907

1906 Austrian physician Clemens von Pirquet shows that hay fever is an allergic reaction to pollen and devises the term "allergy."

1907 U.S. zoologist Ross Harrison begins the technique of in vitro tissue culture (growing tissues in glass laboratory apparatus).

1907 German chemist Emil Fischer confirms that proteins are made up of chains of amino acids by synthesizing a polypeptide.

By 1894, French motorists were organizing speed and endurance races.

model steam-powered road vehicle in 1784, and in 1789 U.S. inventor Oliver Evans fitted a high-pressure engine to a four-wheel vehicle. Back in England, Richard Trevithick built a vehicle in 1801 with large driving wheels. It reached a speed of 10 miles (16 km) per hour. In 1829, English inventor Goldsworthy Gurney began a steam coach service, with vehicles averaging a speed of 15 miles (24 km) per hour.

Around 1865, New Yorker Richard Dudgeon built a lightweight steam carriage, and in 1878 French engineer Amédée Bollée's carriage *La Mancelle* had a front-mounted engine driving the rear wheels. It traveled at up to 25 miles (40 km) per hour. However, just as they became efficient, steam carriages declined in the face of competition from the railroads.

The Gasoline Engine

The next step came from Germans Karl Benz and Gottlieb Daimler. They saw the potential of the gasoline engine. Benz's first three-wheel car dates from 1885. Its 1-horsepower engine reached 8 miles (13 km) per hour.

TIMELINE
1908–1909

KEY:

- Astronomy and Math
- Biology and Medicine
- Chemistry and Physics
- Engineering and Invention

1908

1908 Danish astronomer Ejnar Hertzsprung introduces a method of classifying stars by plotting a graph of luminosity against temperature.

1908 The first Model T Ford comes off the assembly line in Detroit, Michigan.

1908 The Tunguska event occurs in Siberia; it may have been a comet colliding with Earth.

1908 U.S. physicist William Coolidge uses tungsten to make an incandescent filament lamp.

1908 French anthropologist Marcellin Boule reconstructs the first complete Neanderthal skeleton.

1908 U.S. inventor Elmer Sperry produces a gyroscope for ships.

Henry Ford's Assembly Line

Henry Ford's vision was to make the car available to all Americans by reducing the cost. He brought in a system in which the car chassis moved slowly along while workers repeated the same task on every chassis. A car could now be made in 1 hour 33 minutes, rather than the 12 hours it had taken before. Ford paid his workers better than average wages to keep his workforce stable. By 1914, one of Ford's own workers could buy a Model T with four months' pay.

Daimler built his first car in 1886, with a gasoline engine in a heavier four-wheel vehicle. By 1891, French engineers René Panhard and Émile Levassor had front-mounted Daimler engines to drive rear wheels. They had modern steering, a gear box, and a friction clutch. By 1893, Benz was making the more stable four-wheel cars with 3-horsepower engines. The same year, U.S. inventors Charles and Frank Duryea built the first gasoline-engine car. The first U.S.-made auto (Duryea) went on sale in 1896.

Industrialist Henry Ford revolutionized carmaking by introducing mass-production techniques at the start of the 20th century. As a chassis moved slowly along an assembly line, workers added different parts to it. In 1908, the method produced the Model T, or "Tin Lizzy," as it was known. "You can have it in any color as long as it's black," declared Ford. The motor age was born.

⟩⟩ The Model T had high axles to cope with rough, unsurfaced rural roads and tracks.

1909 Danish chemist Søren Sørensen introduces the concept of pH, which measures hydrogen ion concentration to reveal the strength of an acid or alkali.

1909 French aviator Louis Blériot flies across the English Channel.

1909 Danish botanist Wilhelm Johannsen coins the term "gene" for the factor that carries inheritable characteristics.

1909

1909 English physiologist Henry Dale discovers oxytocin, the hormone that controls the womb during childbirth.

1909 "SOS" is introduced as the international radio distress signal.

1909 Russian-born U.S. chemist Phoebus Levene identifies the sugar ribose in some nucleic acids (now known as RNA, ribonucleic acid).

The Airplane

Even before the invention of flying machines, people wanted to imitate birds and take to the air. It was not until the 20th century that the ambition was realized.

➤➤ The Wright Brothers' *Flyer* was a glider with an engine attached for power.

TIMELINE 1910–1912

KEY:

- Astronomy and Math
- Biology and Medicine
- Chemistry and Physics
- Engineering and Invention

1910 New-Zealand born English physicist Ernest Rutherford proves the existence of the atom.

1910 French engineer Henri Fabre builds the first seaplane.

1911 Dutch physicist Heike Kamerlingh Onnes discovers superconductivity, the total loss of electrical resistance that some substances have at very low temperatures.

1910

1911

1910 U.S. pathologist Francis Rous identifies the first cancer-causing virus.

1910 U.S. airman Eugene Fly makes the first airplane flight off the deck of a ship.

1911 English physiologist Henry Dale identifies histamine, a substance released by the body to fight allergies.

Timeline
1808 Unmanned glider

1848 Steam-powered model airplane

1853 Human-carrying glider

1890 Unmanned steam-powered airplane

1891 Steerable human-carrying glider

1903 Sustained flight in gasoline-engined airplane

The first heavier-than-air machines to fly were kites, invented by the Chinese around 1000 B.C. By the late 19th century, human-carrying kites were built. English soldier Baden Baden-Powell designed one in 1894, and American showman "Colonel" Samuel Cody improved it in 1901. But real progress did not come until people began to experiment with gliders.

Off the Ground

The first person to build a steerable glider that could be controlled in flight was German Otto Lilienthal. His first manned flight was made in 1891. His early machines copied birds' wings, but later he added a tail for stability and came up with the idea of two pairs of wings. The two-wing arrangement, later called a biplane, remained a feature of nearly all early flying machines. In the United States, Wilbur Wright and his brother Orville read about Lilienthal's pioneering work, which would influence their experiments. By 1903, they had perfected their human-carrying gliders.

→ Otto Lilienthal makes his first glider flight in 1891. He later died in a glider crash.

Powered Flight

By the early 20th century, engineers had an "airframe." Now all they needed was a suitable power source. At the time, the steam engine was the only possibility.

1912 The largest extant lizard, the Komodo dragon, is discovered in Indonesia.

1912 Grand Central Station—the largest railroad station in the world—is completed in New York.

1912

1911 German physicist Karl Ferdinand Braun devises a scanning system for cathode-ray tubes, later used for TV and radar.

1912 The SS *Titanic* sinks on its first voyage, with the loss of 1,489 lives.

1912 German chemist Paul Ehrlich introduces acriflavine for use as an antiseptic.

The Wright *Flyer*

The Wright brothers' *Flyer* used a light aluminum gasoline engine to power two "pusher" propellers. The propellers rotated in opposite directions to keep torque from rotating the whole airplane. The pilot steered using a combination of the rudder and "wing warping." This involved flexing the ends of the wings (like a bird) to bank the plane into a turn. The pilot used the elevator to make it climb and descend. After several flights, with the brothers taking turns as pilot, the plane was damaged. It never flew again.

Various inventors tried their hands at flying steam-powered mono- and biplanes, but none succeeded in flying more than short distances before crashing. Steam engines were just too heavy for the task. The alternative was the gasoline engine. In 1903, Samuel Langley built a full-sized airplane with a gasoline engine. Two attempts failed—the machine crashing into Washington D.C.'s

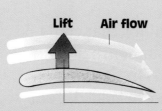

Lift   Air flow

The *Flyer's* wings produced lift because of their shape. Air flowing over the top of the wing has farther to travel and moves faster than the air below. The faster air moves, the lower its pressure. This causes low pressure above the wing and high pressure below it, producing lift.

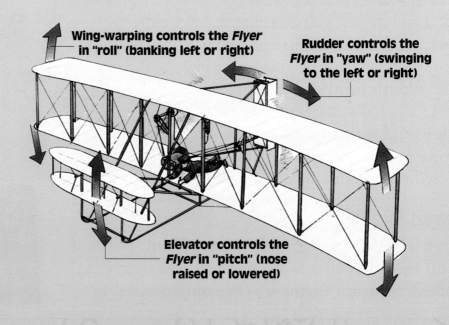

Wing-warping controls the *Flyer* in "roll" (banking left or right)

Rudder controls the *Flyer* in "yaw" (swinging to the left or right)

Elevator controls the *Flyer* in "pitch" (nose raised or lowered)

TIMELINE
1913–1914

KEY:

- Astronomy and Math
- Biology and Medicine
- Chemistry and Physics
- Engineering and Invention

1913

1913 U.S. physicist William Coolidge invents the X-ray tube.

1913 U.S. chemist William Burton patents a method for "cracking" crude oil by breaking it down into simpler compounds using heat.

1913 U.S. biochemists discover Vitamin A.

1913 French physicist Charles Fabry reveals the existence of the ozone layer in Earth's upper atmosphere.

1913 Danish physicist Niels Bohr proposes a model of the atom in which negatively charged electrons orbit a positively charged neutron.

Potomac River. The Wright brothers built their own gasoline engine out of lightweight aluminum and attached it to one of their gliders. The launch of this machine at Kitty Hawk, North Carolina, on December 17, 1903 heralded the start of sustained heavier-than-air flight. For the first time, a human flew in a machine that took off and landed under full control. It was three years before another airplane succeeded—in 1906, Brazilian aviator Alberto Santos-Dumont made short flights in a motorized glider of his own design.

The next advances mainly involved materials. Steel and other alloys replaced wood for airframes, and aluminum panels instead of varnished cloth were used to cover them. Jets superseded gasoline engines, and just 44 years after the Wright brothers' first flight, an airplane flew faster than the speed of sound.

↑ French aviator Louis Blériot's airplane lies on the ground near Dover, United Kingdom, after his flight from France in 1909—the first long flight over a body of water.

1914 U.S. psychologist John Watson proposes that experimental animals can be used to study human psychology.

1914 English military engineer Ernest Swinton proposes building the tank.

1914 German engineer Oskar Barnack produces a prototype Leica camera.

1914

1914 English astronomer Arthur Eddington recognizes that nebulas are galaxies made up of millions of stars.

1914 The 40-mile (64-km) Panama Canal is completed between the Atlantic and Pacific Oceans.

1914 U.S. inventor Garrett Morgan produces a practical gas mask.

Synthetic Drugs

The mid- to late 19th century saw chemists declare war on pain. Some developments came from traditional medicines, others came from experiments, and a few were luck.

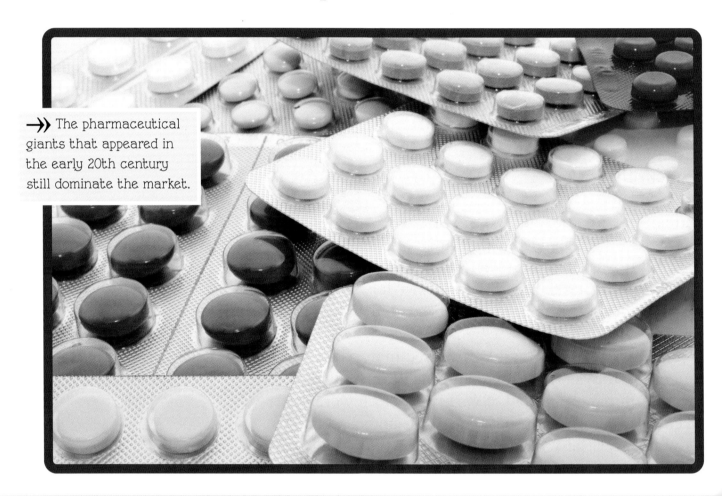

→》 The pharmaceutical giants that appeared in the early 20th century still dominate the market.

TIMELINE
1915–1917

KEY:

- Astronomy and Math
- Biology and Medicine
- Chemistry and Physics
- Engineering and Invention

1915

1915 U.S. astronomer Walter Adams identifies Sirius B as the first white dwarf star.

1915 English inventor William Mills invents the Mills bomb, a type of hand grenade used during World War I.

1915 The German company Junkers makes the first all-metal, cantilever-wing airplane, the Junkers J–1.

1915 U.S. surgeon Alexis Carrel performs open-heart surgery on a dog.

1915 Bacteriologists independently discover viruses that attack bacteria.

1915 Scottish astronomer Robert Innes locates Proxima Centauri, the star nearest the sun.

Humans have used naturally occurring substances as medicines for thousands of years. Some of them, such as opiates, were used as analgesics (painkillers); but they were never very reliable, and they often had undesirable side effects.

The First Synthetic Drugs

The first totally synthetic drugs were gases. In 1799, English chemist Humphry Davy discovered the painkilling properties of nitrous oxide, also known as laughing gas. In 1815, similar properties were noted for ether vapor. But amazingly, it was another 30 years before medical practitioners were to take advantage of their painkilling properties to perform surgery. In 1847, a stronger anesthetic gas, chloroform vapor, was developed by Scottish obstetrician James Simpson and used to help women during childbirth. None of the gases were free from side effects, notably that they made the patient unconscious, or at least insensible, and they were poisonous in large doses.

CONTAINS 100 TABLETS

TABLETS

ON TONIC FOR THE BLOO

Timeline

1799 Laughing gas as painkiller

1815 Ether as painkiller

1828 Salicin isolated from willow

1847 Chloroform used in childbirth

1859 Salicylic acid in mass production

1899 Aspirin launched

1910 Salvarsan 606

← Before modern drugs, people relied on traditional cures or treatments made up and sold by herbalists. Some cures contained naturally occurring drugs that may have had real benefits—but many were useless, and some were actually very harmful.

1916 German-born U.S. physicist Albert Einstein publishes his paper on the general theory of relativity, which mainly concerns gravity.

1917 The 100-inch (2.5-m) telescope is completed at Mount Wilson Observatory near Los Angeles.

1917 U.S. nurse Margaret Sanger opens the first birth control clinic in the United States.

1916

1917

1916 Several scientists make special alloys.

1916 French physicist Paul Langevin produces a primitive form of sonar.

1917 The U.S. Black and Decker company markets the first electric hand drill.

1917 English engineer Archibald Low invents an electronic control system for rockets.

The Wonder Drug

Aspirin is by far the world's most popular synthetic drug. About 30 billion tablets are used every year in the United States. Aspirin forms the basis of many headache and cold cures; it is an anti-inflammatory and reduces fever. It may also help reduce the risk of heart attacks and prevent some kinds of cancer.

The use of certain plants to treat pain and fever has a long history. Ancient Egyptians used myrtle, ancient Greeks and medieval Europeans used willow and meadowsweet, and Native Americans used birch. All these plants contain the same active ingredient, called salicin after the scientific name for willow, *Salix*.

Wonderful Willow

The medicinal use of willow was rediscovered by English clergyman Edward Stone. In 1763, he reported that he had successfully used willow bark to reduce fever in 50 of his patients. The crucial breakthrough came in 1859, when a German chemist, Hermann Kolbe, figured out the chemical structure of salicylic acid and came up with a means of synthesizing it on a large scale—not from plants but from coal tar. Using the Kolbe reaction, the new drug went into mass production.

Salicylic acid was an effective painkiller, but it caused stomachaches, so there was a need to modify the drug. The final steps were made by

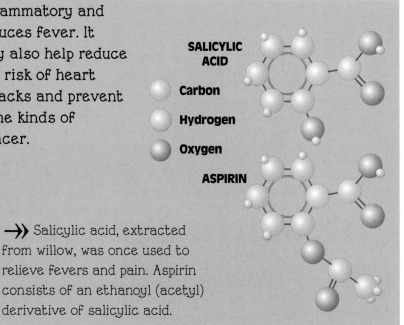

SALICYLIC ACID

○ **Carbon**

○ **Hydrogen**

○ **Oxygen**

ASPIRIN

➔➔ Salicylic acid, extracted from willow, was once used to relieve fevers and pain. Aspirin consists of an ethanoyl (acetyl) derivative of salicylic acid.

TIMELINE
1918–1919

KEY:

▬ Astronomy and Math

▬ Biology and Medicine

▬ Chemistry and Physics

▬ Engineering and Invention

1918 German physical chemist Walther Nernst puts forward a theory of chemical chain reactions.

1918 The world's most powerful radio transmitter begins operations at the naval station in New Brunswick, New Jersey.

1918 U.S. chemist Winford Lewis develops the poison gas lewisite.

1918

1918 U.S. company Kelvinator market the first mechanical refrigerator for home use.

1918 U.S. embryologist Herbert Evans suggests that human body cells have 48 chromosomes each (in fact they have 46).

German chemist Felix Hoffman at the chemical company Bayer. He adapted French chemist Charles Gerhardt's earlier formula to synthesize acetylsalicylic acid, and in 1899 the new drug was launched by Bayer as aspirin. At first, only doctors could administer aspirin, but in 1915 it became available without prescription.

Another drug developed at about the same time as aspirin was phenacetin. It later led to the development of acetaminophen as a painkiller.

Modern Drugs

The therapeutic advancements of the 20th century meant the science of pharmaceutics had finally come of age. The ability to synthesize new compounds and tinker with their structure to modify their pharmacological effects is the basis of almost all modern drug development and is continually undergoing further adaptations.

↓ Willow is just one natural source of salicin; the chemical occurs in plants discovered and used independently by ancient peoples around the world.

1919 U.S. astronomer Edwin Hubble begins his long study of Cepheid variable stars in the Andromeda Galaxy.

1919 Austrian zoologist Karl von Frisch describes the "dance" by which bees communicate with one another.

1919 U.S. psychologist John Watson suggests that behavioral conditioning should be a subject of psychological research.

1919

1919 English physicist Francis Aston develops the mass spectroscope for separating isotopes.

1919 New Zealand-born English physicist Ernest Rutherford reports that he has disintegrated nitrogen atoms by bombarding them with alpha particles.

1919 British aviators John Alcock and Arthur Brown make the first nonstop flight across the Atlantic.

Subatomic Particles

By 1920, physicists knew every atom consists of a nucleus
carrying a positive electromagnetic charge surrounded by
a cloud of electrons carrying a negative charge.

→》 The paths of
subatomic particles
are traced through a
cloud chamber.

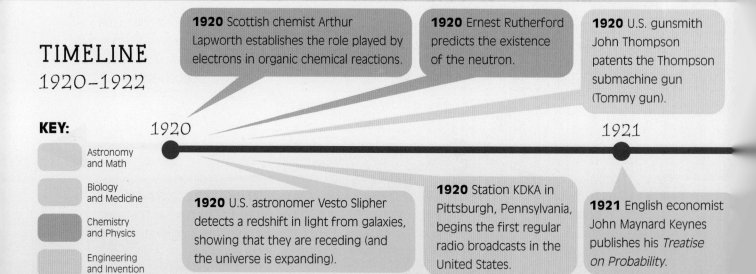

TIMELINE
1920–1922

KEY:

- Astronomy
  and Math
- Biology
  and Medicine
- Chemistry
  and Physics
- Engineering
  and Invention

1920 Scottish chemist Arthur
Lapworth establishes the role played by
electrons in organic chemical reactions.

1920 Ernest Rutherford
predicts the existence
of the neutron.

1920 U.S. gunsmith
John Thompson
patents the Thompson
submachine gun
(Tommy gun).

1920

1921

1920 U.S. astronomer Vesto Slipher
detects a redshift in light from galaxies,
showing that they are receding (and
the universe is expanding).

1920 Station KDKA in
Pittsburgh, Pennsylvania,
begins the first regular
radio broadcasts in the
United States.

1921 English economist
John Maynard Keynes
publishes his *Treatise
on Probability*.

E rnest Rutherford, the New Zealand-born English physicist, found that when he bombarded nitrogen atoms with alpha particles (helium nuclei), hydrogen nuclei were released. In 1920, Rutherford suggested the name "proton" (from the Greek *protos*, meaning "first") for the hydrogen nucleus.

Smashing Particles

Rutherford's research continued to center on smashing atomic nuclei by bombarding them with alpha particles. In 1925, English physicist Patrick Blackett, working under him, developed the cloud chamber into a device for recording the disintegration of atoms. But alpha particles were not powerful enough to smash large nuclei, which repelled them without disintegrating. More energetic impacts were needed, and in 1932, English physicist John Cockcroft and Irish physicist Ernest Walton built the world's first particle accelerator at the Cavendish Laboratory. It used powerful

Timeline

1920 Proton named

1925 Cloud chamber invented in 1911 developed further

1932 First antimatter particle, positron, discovered; neutron identified

1934 Neutrino identified and named

1937 Muon discovered

⟵ Ernest Rutherford oversaw much of the early research into subatomic particles. However, the major breakthrough relied on the development of particle accelerators to create more powerful collisions between particles.

1921 Canadian physiologist Frederick Banting isolates insulin, the hormone that controls glucose levels in the blood.

1921 U.S. airman John MacReady demonstrates spraying crops from an airplane.

1922 The BBC—British Broadcasting Company (later Corporation)—begins regular broadcasts in London.

1922

1921 The first expressway (Autobahn) opens in Germany.

1922 U.S. anatomist Herbert Evans discovers vitamin E.

1922 A Scottish team first use insulin to treat patients with diabetes.

1922 German chemist Hermann Staudinger recognizes that substances such as rubber are natural polymers.

electromagnets to accelerate protons that were then directed at a target.

Nature of Radiation

In 1932, French physicists Irène and Frédéric Joliot-Curie found that alpha bombardment of paraffins or similar hydrocarbons (compounds of hydrogen and carbon) led to the emission of protons with very high energy. English physicist James Chadwick, working at the Cavendish Laboratory, conducted experiments which suggested that this high-energy radiation consisted of particles with approximately the same mass as the proton, but carrying no electromagnetic charge.

Chadwick thought the new particle was a proton bound to an electron (a hydrogen atom), and he was able to calculate the mass of the particle. Because it carries no charge, unlike electrons, the particle came to be called the "neutron."

↑ Scientists check part of the Large Hadron Collider, which shoots particles around a 17-mile (27-km) underground loop in Switzerland.

TIMELINE
1923–1924

KEY:

- Astronomy and Math
- Biology and Medicine
- Chemistry and Physics
- Engineering and Invention

1923

1923 Austrian doctor Sigmund Freud introduces his theory of the subconscious mind.

1923 Scottish engineer John Logie Baird invents a television system that uses mechanical scanning.

1923 Austro-Hungarian rocket scientist Hermann Oberth introduces the idea of escape velocity, the speed needed to leave Earth's gravity.

1923 U.S. physical chemist Gilbert Lewis defines an acid as a substance that accepts electrons.

1923 U.S. physicians George and Gladys Dick isolate the bacteria that cause scarlet fever.

1923 The German Benz company makes the first trucks with diesel engines.

In 1930, Wolfgang Pauli—one of the greatest physicists of the 20th century—was studying beta radiation, a stream of electrons emitted by unstable atoms. The electrons seemed to lose energy, but no explanation could be found for the loss. Pauli's solution was to propose that beta radiation also contains a previously unknown particle with the unusual properties of possessing no charge and no mass when it is at rest. The particle was later named the "neutrino."

During the late 1920s, theoretical physicists were very interested in the properties of electrons. American physicist Carl Anderson discovered the particle later called "positron" in 1932, as did Patrick Blackett in 1933. It was the first antimatter particle to be identified.

➤➤ Cockcroft and Walton's atom splitter was the world's first particle accelerator.

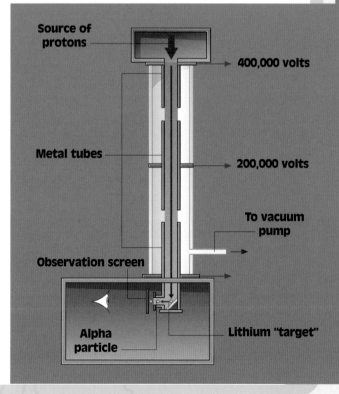

Source of protons

400,000 volts

Metal tubes

200,000 volts

To vacuum pump

Observation screen

Alpha particle

Lithium "target"

Building the Atom Splitter

In 1932, John Cockcroft and Ernest Walton charged a hollow metal chamber to 400,000 volts and injected protons into it. The positively charged particles were driven away from the high positive voltage along a series of tubes kept at lower voltages. They struck a piece of lithium. Alpha particles (helium nuclei) that were formed in the interaction caused flashes on an observation screen and were then photographed.

1924 English watchmaker John Harwood patents a self-winding wristwatch.

1924 A team of U.S. pilots make the first round-the-world flight (they stop only to refuel).

1924 English physicist Edward Appleton uses radio waves to demonstrate the existence of the ionosphere, a layer of ionized gases in the upper atmosphere.

1924

1924 The Computing-Tabulating-Recording Company changes its name to International Business Machines (IBM).

1924 Swedish chemist Theodor Svedberg builds the ultracentrifuge.

1924 Australian anthropologist Raymond Dart discovers fossils of *Australopithecus* in Africa. They help establish Africa as the site of humanity's origins.

The First Television

In October 1925, Scottish electrical engineer John Logie Baird transmitted the first television pictures in his London workshop.

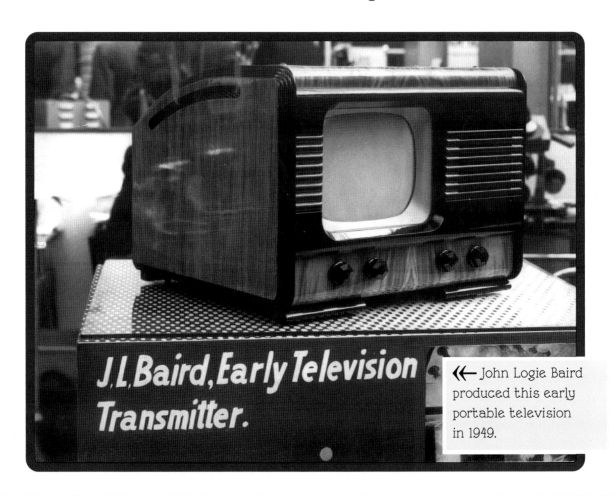

J.L.Baird, Early Television Transmitter.

←← John Logie Baird produced this early portable television in 1949.

TIMELINE
1925–1927

KEY:

- Astronomy and Math
- Biology and Medicine
- Chemistry and Physics
- Engineering and Invention

1925 English physicist Patrick Blackett begins experiments with colliding atoms in a cloud chamber.

1925 African American biologist Ernest Just shows that UV radiation can cause cancer.

1926 U.S. physical chemist Gilbert Lewis coins the word photon to describe a quantum, or particle, of light.

1925

1926

1925 U.S. pathologist George Whipple discovers iron in red blood cells.

1925 U.S. astronomer Edwin Hubble introduces a classification scheme for galaxies.

1926 U.S. geneticist Hermann Muller produces genetic mutations in fruit flies by exposing them to radiation.

John Logie Baird was born in the west of Scotland and educated in Glasgow. His poor health cost him his job as an electrical engineer, and after three failed businesses he retired to live in the southern English coastal town of Hastings in 1922. It was there that he began experimenting with television.

↑ Baird poses with his early apparatus, including a Nipkov disk with a spiral of holes that scan an image as a series of lines as the disk rotates.

Capturing an Image

All television cameras require some method of scanning an image. Baird used a rapidly spinning Nipkov disk patented by Polish electrical engineer Paul Nipkov in 1884. It is a disk—Baird's was made from cardboard—pierced with a spiral of holes. As the disk rotates, an observer looking through it sees an object as a series of curved lines or scans, each of which is produced by a different hole in the disk. The first pictures of 1925 depicted a ventriloquist's doll named Stooky Bill. The first live subject (in 1926) was an office boy who worked in the premises below Baird's London workshop.

Timeline

1923 Zworykin invents iconoscope TV camera tube

1925 Baird's first television pictures

1929 BBC begins experimental TV broadcasts

1937 BBC begins commercial TV broadcasts

1938 Zworykin receives patent for iconoscope TV camera tube

1941 CBS begins experimental color TV broadcasts

1926 Norwegian inventor Erik Rotheim invents the aerosol can.

1927 English zoologist Charles Elton publishes *Animal Ecology*, which establishes the science of ecology.

1927 English chemist Nevil Sidgwick introduces the modern theory of chemical valence, about the role of electrons in chemical bonds.

1927

1926 U.S. inventor Robert Goddard successfully launches a liquid-fuel rocket.

1927 German theoretical physicist Werner Heisenberg formulates his uncertainty principle.

1927 U.S. aviator Charles Lindbergh makes the first solo flight across the Atlantic Ocean.

The First TV Camera

The iconoscope was developed by Vladimir Zworykin in 1923 (patented 1938). An electron beam from an electron gun scans an image focused onto a photosensitive plate. Deflection plates make the electron beam scan in lines from side to side. Light striking the plate gives it a positive charge. Electrons not held by the charge bounce to another electrode and form the video signal.

➡️ Zworykin's iconoscope was the first successful television camera tube.

At first, Baird sent his television images along wires. By 1927, he transmitted pictures along a telephone line, and a year later he sent pictures over the Atlantic telegraph cable to New York.

In September 1929, the British Broadcasting Corporation (BBC) began experimental television broadcasts using Baird's mechanical system. The flickering images consisted of only 30 lines, later increased to 60 and eventually 240 lines. In 1932, Baird transmitted pictures by shortwave radio. The experimental broadcasts ended in 1935. By the time commercial television broadcasting started in Britain in 1937, the BBC had adopted the 405-line electronic system developed by the British company Marconi-EMI. But World War II stopped television broadcasting. Before the end of the war, Baird had produced color television and three-dimensional images as well as a widescreen

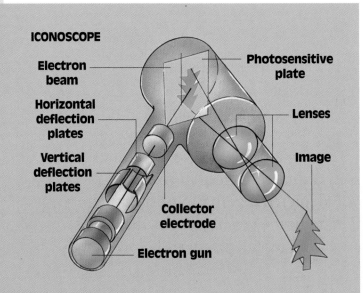

ICONOSCOPE

Electron beam

Horizontal deflection plates

Vertical deflection plates

Photosensitive plate

Lenses

Image

Collector electrode

Electron gun

TIMELINE
1928–1929

KEY:

- Astronomy and Math
- Biology and Medicine
- Chemistry and Physics
- Engineering and Invention

1928

1928 U.S. astronomer Henry Russell determines that hydrogen is the most abundant element in the sun's atmosphere.

1928 U.S. mathematician John von Neumann outlines the foundations of game theory.

1928 U.S. aviator Amelia Earhart becomes the first woman to fly the Atlantic.

1928 English theoretical physicist Paul Dirac predicts the existence of antimatter particles.

1928 Scottish bacteriologist Alexander Fleming discovers the antibiotic penicillin.

1928 U.S. inventor Jacob Schick patents the electric razor.

system (by projection) and stereophonic sound. He died before television broadcasting resumed. When it started again, it used an all-electronic system.

Electronic Systems

Scottish engineer Alan Campbell-Swinton figured out the principles of an electronic system in 1908, although at that time the apparatus was not available to put his ideas into practice. In the United States, Russian-born Vladimir Zworykin went the electronic route from the start with his iconoscope. U.S. inventor Philo Farnsworth developed a similar camera in 1927. Zworykin joined RCA and soon improved his system. In 1941, CBS made experimental color broadcasts from Station WCBW in New York, although regular transmissions in color did not begin until 1951.

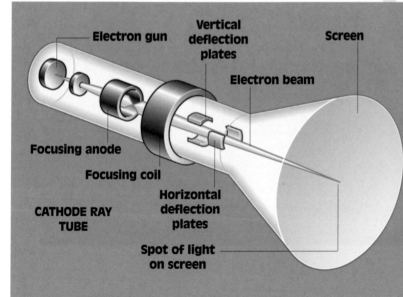

Electron gun

Vertical deflection plates

Screen

Electron beam

Focusing anode

Focusing coil

Horizontal deflection plates

CATHODE RAY TUBE

Spot of light on screen

The Cathode Ray Tube

The cathode ray tube, invented in 1897 by German physicist Ferdinand Braun, is the heart of a television receiver. Like the iconoscope, it has an electron gun and deflection plates and a coil to focus the electron beam onto the screen at the front. A phosphor, which gives off light when struck by electrons, coats the inside of the screen on which the scanned image builds up line by line.

⇐ The screen of the cathode ray tube is coated with chemicals called phosphors.

1929 German biochemist Adolf Butenandt isolates the female sex hormone estrogen.

1929 German-born U.S. physicist Albert Einstein announces his unified field theory, which attempts to bring all the fundamental forces into a single theory.

1929 Japanese geophysicist Motonori Matuyama suggests that Earth's magnetic field has undergone reversals several times in its history.

1929

1929 German engineer Felix Wankel patents his rotary engine.

1929 A German Zeppelin airship makes a 21-day around-the-world flight.

1929 U.S. astronomer Edwin Hubble formulates a law that relates the distance of a star to the speed with which it moves away from Earth.

Penicillin and Antibiotics

In the early part of the 20th century, millions of people died each year from bacterial infections. But the discovery of a mold that could kill germs would change all that.

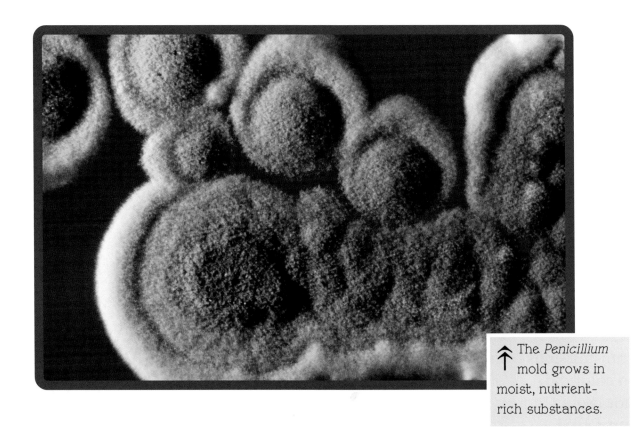

↑ The *Penicillium* mold grows in moist, nutrient-rich substances.

TIMELINE
1930–1932

KEY:
- Astronomy and Math
- Biology and Medicine
- Chemistry and Physics
- Engineering and Invention

1930 English engineer Frank Whittle invents the gas turbine (jet) engine.

1930 U.S. businessman Clarence Birdseye markets the first quick-frozen foods.

1930 Austrian-born Swiss physicist Wolfgang Pauli predicts the existence of the neutrino.

1930

1931

1930 U.S. astronomer Clyde Tombaugh discovers the planet Pluto (now classed as a dwarf planet).

1930 U.S. engineer Vannevar Bush builds an analog computer.

1930 U.S. chemist Wallace Carothers discovers neoprene, leading to the production of nylon.

From the late 19th century, thanks to the work of French chemist Louis Pasteur and others, scientists and medical practitioners recognized a new type of enemy—bacteria, or "germs." Many bacteria had been identified, and the conditions they caused in humans were better understood.

Discovery of Penicillin

Wound infection was the specialized area of Scottish bacteriologist Alexander Fleming. Unlike other medical researchers of the time, Fleming believed that the way to tackle infection was to harness natural processes to destroy infection through biological cures.

In 1928, after returning from vacation to his laboratory in London, Fleming noticed something unusual about a culture of *Staphylococcus* bacteria that he had left developing in a petri dish. In his absence, a mold had grown in the dish, and it appeared to be killing the *Staphylococcus*. Fleming identified the strange mold as a species of *Penicillium* and discovered that the liquid it produced (penicillin) was just as effective at destroying a large number of

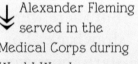
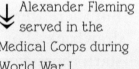
Alexander Fleming served in the Medical Corps during World War I.

Timeline

1877 Pasteur observes anthrax-killing bacteria

1921 Fleming discovers lysozyme in living cells

1928 Fleming identifies penicillin

1940 Mice and humans treated with penicillin

c.1943 Penicillin in mass production

1931 U.S. pathologist Ernest Goodpasture devises a way of growing viruses in chicken eggs.

1931 U.S. chemist Linus Pauling explains the nature of benzene.

1932 British and Irish physicists carry out the first nuclear fission.

1932 U.S. physicist Ernest Lawrence operates the first cyclotron, one of the first particle accelerators.

1932

1931 U.S. radio engineer Karl Jansky accidentally discovers radio waves from space, leading to the science of radio astronomy.

1932 Synthetic rubber is first marketed in the United States under the name Duprene.

1932 The Sydney Harbor Bridge is completed in Australia.

"Antibiotic" means "destroyer of life:" antibiotics destroy the bacteria causing illness. In 1877, Louis Pasteur noticed that anthrax cultures died when mixed with other bacteria. In 1889, Frenchman Paul Vuillemin named the process by which one organism kills another "antibiosis." From that came the word "antibiotic," first used by U.S. biochemist Selman Waksman in 1941. He received a Nobel Prize in 1952 for his discovery of Streptomycin, the first successful treatment for tuberculosis.

different bacteria. More exciting still, it appeared to have no effect on healthy living tissue, so Fleming thought it could be safe to use on humans. But there were drawbacks. For a start, there were several disease-causing bacteria—notably those responsible for plague and cholera—on which it had no effect at all. Even more disheartening was the fact that penicillin turned out to be very difficult to produce.

Fleming's work was followed up by an international team of scientists.

Manufacturing Penicillin

The problems seemed insurmountable at first, but in 1939, a group of scientists at Oxford University in England began following up Fleming's discovery. The team was led by Australian pathologist Howard Florey and German biochemist Ernst Chain. By 1940, they extracted penicillin and began testing it on mice. A dose of penicillin enabled mice to fight off infections that

TIMELINE
1933–1934

KEY:

- Astronomy and Math
- Biology and Medicine
- Chemistry and Physics
- Engineering and Invention

1933

1933 English engineer Alan Blumlein patents a system of stereophonic sound recording.

1933 The Boeing 247, the first modern airliner, goes into service.

1933 Polish and English chemists synthesize vitamin C, the first vitamin to be artificially produced.

1933 Swiss astrophysicist Fritz Zwicky suggests that space must contain invisible "dark matter" (to explain the total mass of the universe).

1933 English aviator Alan Cobham devises a system for refueling airplanes in flight.

1933 The Tasmanian wolf becomes extinct in the wild.

otherwise would have killed them. Thanks to refinements in the production technique developed by English biochemist Norman Heatley, the "miracle" drug was being mass-produced in the United States and Britain by about 1943.

The development could not have come at a more crucial time. World War II was raging, and wounded servicemen were the first to benefit. Thousands of lives were saved, at least on the Allied Forces' side. After the war, the benefits of penicillin were spread more widely. Fleming, Florey, and Chain received the 1945 Nobel Prize for Medicine. Heatley was recognized by an honorary degree from Oxford University in 1990.

↓ Penicillin saved many lives at field hospitals that treated wounded soldiers during World War II.

1934 Astrophysicists studying supernovas predict the existence of neutron stars.

1934 U.S. scientist Royal Raymond Rife tests a cancer-curing treatment using radio waves.

1934 In France, Citroën launches the first mass-produced, front-wheel-drive car.

1934

1934 Dutch physicist Hendrik Casimir explains the phenomenon of superconductivity.

1934 English inventor Percy Shaw patents "cats eyes," reflecting road markers.

1934 U.S. psychologist B. F. Skinner invents the Skinner box for studying the psychology of animals.

The Development of Radar

During the 1920s and 1930s, researchers realized that radio reflection could provide a way of detecting planes and other objects such as ships and icebergs.

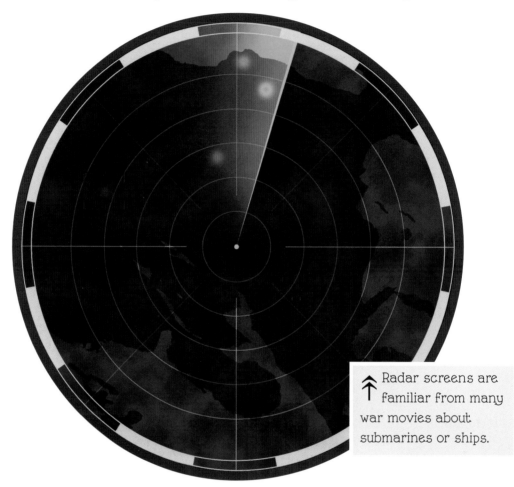

↑ Radar screens are familiar from many war movies about submarines or ships.

TIMELINE
1935–1937

KEY:

- Astronomy and Math
- Biology and Medicine
- Chemistry and Physics
- Engineering and Invention

1935 U.S. seismologist devises the Richter scale to measure earthquake intensity.

1935 Portuguese neurologist António de Egas Moniz introduces prefrontal lobotomy as a treatment for some personality disorders.

1936 Danish seismologist Inge Lehmann suggests that Earth's inner core is solid and surrounded by liquid metal.

1935

1936

1935 U.S. amateur photographers invent Kodachrome transparency film.

1935 U.S. chemist Robert Williams announces the structure of vitamin B1.

1935 U.S. physicist Arthur Dempster discovers the isotope uranium-235. It is later used in atom bombs.

↑ In 1904, Christian Hülsmeyer patented a primitive radar system to warn ships of obstructions.

R adar stands for "radio detecting and ranging," which explains exactly what the process does. To detect a plane, a radar set transmits a pulse of very high-frequency radio waves (microwaves), and a receiving antenna picks up any radio echoes that return. The direction of the returning signal reveals the direction of any target present, and its range can be calculated from the time it takes for the microwave signal to travel out and back.

The First Steps

In 1904, German engineer Christian Hülsmeyer took out the first patents for such a device. He planned a system that used continuous waves (not radio pulses) to warn ships of possible collisions. In 1922, engineers at the U.S. Naval Research Laboratory in Washington, D.C., sent radio signals across the Potomac River and detected passing ships when they interrupted the radio beam. In Britain, Scottish physicist Robert Watson-Watt was

Timeline

1904 Christian Hülsmeyer's patent

1921 Magnetron

1939 Cavity magnetron

1922 U.S. Naval Research Laboratory experiments

1935 Robert Watson-Watt's patent

1938 Klystron

1939 Cavity magnetron

1939 Lawrence Hyland's demonstration

1936 The British Supermarine Spitfire fighter airplane makes its maiden flight.

1937 U.S. electrical engineer George Stibitz makes a binary adding machine.

1937 The Golden Gate Bridge is completed in San Francisco.

1937 The Swiss company Nestlé begins selling instant coffee (Nescafé).

1937

1936 The first giant panda is captured alive in the wild.

1937 Swiss-born Italian pharmacologist Daniel Bovet identifies the first antihistamine substance that is effective in treating allergies.

1937 U.S. physicist Chester Carlson invents xerography, a dry photocopying process.

The Cavity Magnetron

A cavity magnetron is at the heart of microwave devices, including radar. Inside a block of conductive material (the anode block) is a filament that generates electrons. The electrons are concentrated into a cloud by a magnetic field. As the cloud passes vanes inside the anode block, the electric charges generate a vibrating electromagnetic field. An antenna picks up the vibrations, which travel out through a waveguide as microwaves.

asked to investigate the use of radio beams as "death rays" to attack enemy pilots. Using a BBC transmitter, he detected a Heyford bomber flying 7 miles (11 km) away at a height of 9,800 feet (3,000 m). By September 1938, with war approaching, the British built a chain of radar antennas on towers 330 feet (100 m) high along the eastern and southern coastlines of England. They detected incoming airplanes at a range of up to 200 miles (320 km).

Engineers also adapted radars to aim guns, particularly antiaircraft guns and (in Germany) long-range naval guns. In the United States, Canadian-born engineer Lawrence Hyland renewed official interest in antiaircraft and aircraft-detection radars, demonstrating a system on the USS *New York* in 1939.

Later Advances

The very high frequencies of radar signals require special electronics. Early transmitters used a

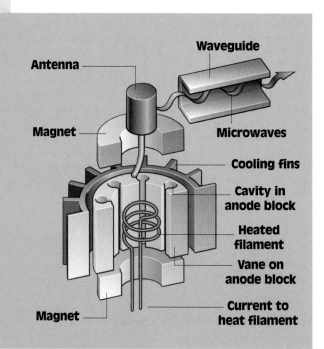

Labels for the cavity magnetron diagram:
- Antenna
- Magnet
- Waveguide
- Microwaves
- Cooling fins
- Cavity in anode block
- Heated filament
- Vane on anode block
- Current to heat filament
- Magnet

TIMELINE
1938–1939

KEY:

- Astronomy and Math
- Biology and Medicine
- Chemistry and Physics
- Engineering and Invention

1938

1938 The asteroid Hermes approaches closer to Earth than any previous observed asteroid: 485,000 miles (780,000 km).

1938 German physicists induce nuclear fission in uranium.

1938 German engineer Ferdinand Porsche designs the Volkswagen "Beetle" car.

1938 U.S. chemist Roy Plunkett synthesizes the "nonstick" plastic PTFE (Teflon).

1938 South African professor J. L. B. Smith identifies a coelacanth, a fish previously thought to be extinct.

1938 Hungarian-born Argentine inventor Laslo Biró makes a prototype of the first ballpoint pen.

vacuum tube called a magnetron. An improved version came in about 1934 from the French company CSF, invented by Henri Gutton. Two researchers at Birmingham University, John Randall and Henry Boot, developed a new device in 1939. It generated wavelengths as small as 3.5 inches (9 cm), and a radar using it could detect a submarine periscope 7 miles (11 km) away. The British government immediately gave details of this "cavity magnetron" (see box on page 36) to researchers in the United States.

After World War II, radar found a wide range of peacetime applications, such as air traffic control and ship navigation. In 1946, astronomers picked up radar signals reflected back from the moon, and in 1958 echoes came back from the planet Venus. NASA has used probes to map the bottom of Earth's oceans and the surface of Venus. Weather forecasters use satellite radar, as do many law enforcement agencies to catch speeding motorists.

↓ Modern radar antennae sometimes resemble golf balls. This one guides aircraft toward an airport runway.

1939 U.S. physicist John Atanasoff makes a prototype electronic binary calculator.

1939 U.S. physicist Albert Einstein tells President F. D. Roosevelt that the discovery of nuclear chain reactions would lead to the building of bombs.

1939 U.S. zoologist Victor Shelford introduces the concept of biomes (major geographical areas that support their own range of organisms).

1939

1939 French chemist Marguerite Perey discovers the radioactive element francium.

1939 The National Broadcasting Company (NBC) begins regular TV transmissions in the United States.

1939 Swiss chemist Paul Müller realizes the insect-killing properties of DDT.

Wernher von Braun

Wernher von Braun was a German-trained engineer and pioneer rocket scientist who became an American citizen and worked on NASA's successful space program.

⟹ The V-2 rocket represented the pinnacle of von Braun's achievements.

TIMELINE
1940–1942

KEY:

Astronomy and Math

Biology and Medicine

Chemistry and Physics

Engineering and Invention

1940

1941

1940 Three heavy radioactive elements are identified, including plutonium, by U.S. physical chemist Glenn Seaborg.

1940 The Tacoma Narrows suspension bridge in Washington State collapses because of oscillation.

1941 German computer pioneer Konrad Zuse completes his third computer (the Z3).

1940 British and Australian scientists extract and purify penicillin and perform the first clinical trials of the drug.

1940 U.S. zoologist Donald Griffin announces that bats "echolocate" using ultrasound.

1941 Soviet nuclear physicists observe spontaneous nuclear fission in uranium.

As a boy, Wernher von Braun read science fiction by Jules Verne and H. G. Wells. He studied engineering at Berlin and Zurich universities. From 1930, he made experimental rockets for the German Society for Space Travel. Rocket testing was banned in Germany under the terms of the Versailles Treaty (signed in 1918 after World War I), so he worked on ballistics. The ballistics and munitions branch of the German army, led by rocket engineer Walter Dornberger, noticed his activities. With the backing of Adolf Hitler, von Braun went to the newly established rocket research center at Peenemünde on the Baltic Sea coast, where in 1936 he became director.

The Vengeance Weapon

At Peenemünde, von Braun's greatest achievement was the "vengeance weapon" 2 (V-2). Originally designed by Dornberger in 1941 as the A-4, the huge rocket used liquid oxygen and alcohol as fuel, weighed over 11 tons, and delivered a warhead containing 1.1 tons of explosives. Its launch speed of 2,500 feet (760 m) per second carried it high into the upper atmosphere, then it came down silently toward a target 200 miles (320 km) away at over three times the speed of sound. Many of the V-2s launched from

⟩⟩ Wernher von Braun (arm in a cast) surrenders to the Americans in 1945.

Timeline

1936 Von Braun director of Peenemünde rocket center

1942 Launch of first A-4 (later V-2) rocket

1946 Von Braun works at White Sands in the U.S.

1958 *Explorer I*, first U.S. satellite

1962 Glenn's orbital flight in *Mercury* capsule

1969 *Apollo* moon landing

1941 English chemists produce the plastic Dacron (Terylene), later licensed to U.S. company DuPont.

1942 Italian-American physicist Enrico Fermi achieves the first controlled nuclear chain reaction, at the University of Chicago.

1942 German rocket engineer Wernher von Braun makes the V-1 and V-2 flying bombs.

1942 French diver Jacques Cousteau invents the aqualung, or scuba.

1942

1941 U.S. biochemist Selman Waksman coins the term "antibiotic" to describe new bacteria-killing drugs.

1942 U.S. radio astronomer Grote Reber compiles the first radio map of the universe.

1942 The Manhattan Project, to make an atom bomb, begins in the United States.

Developing the V-2

The V-2 was the forerunner of all modern rockets. Von Braun based its development on papers written early in the 20th century by the U.S. rocket pioneer Robert Goddard. Its engine was designed to fire for up to 65 seconds, to bring the rocket to the upper reaches of the atmosphere. At that stage, the engine cut out and the rocket angled itself to begin to fall toward its target.

→ Londoners clear wreckage left by one of nearly 1,400 V-2 raids on the British capital.

↑ An American soldier examines a partly built V-2 rocket at the end of World War II.

1944 fell on or around Antwerp in Belgium, and in London.

At the end of the war, von Braun chose to surrender to the U.S. Army and went to the United States. From 1946, he worked at White Sands Proving Ground, New Mexico, and in 1950 moved to the Ballistic Missile Agency at Huntsville, Alabama. There he adapted a V-2 to carry a nuclear warhead, creating the Redstone missile. Von Braun became an American citizen in 1955 and was recruited by the National Aeronautics and Space Administration (NASA). In 1958, he oversaw the successful launch of *Explorer I*, the United States' first

TIMELINE
1943–1944

KEY:

- Astronomy and Math
- Biology and Medicine
- Chemistry and Physics
- Engineering and Invention

1943

1943 U.S. scientists build the world's first operational nuclear reactor at Oak Ridge, Tennessee.

1943 Japanese physicist Sin-Itiro Tomonaga describes the basic physical principles of quantum electrodynamics.

1943 U.S. company Dow Corning is set up to make silicone plastics.

1943 English mathematician Alan Turing oversees the building of Colossus, an electronic stored-program computer for breaking German codes.

1943 Dutch-born U.S. physician Willem Kolff builds the first kidney dialysis machine.

1943 Austrian engineer Paul Eisler makes the first printed circuits for use in electronic devices.

The rockets displayed at the Kennedy Space Center in Florida are all based on Von Braun's basic designs.

artificial satellite. He headed the team that built the *Mercury* capsules for the U. S. manned spaceflight program. In 1960, he became director of the Marshall Space Flight Center, developing the giant three-stage *Saturn V* rocket for NASA's *Apollo* missions. The climax came in 1969, when American astronauts landed on the moon. Von Braun retired from NASA in 1972. He died in 1977.

A Controversial Figure

At the end of the World War II, Werner Von Braun and his team surrendered to the U.S. Army. Von Braun later said that he wanted to make sure that knowledge of the weapon he had created would pass into the right hands. He and his team of technicians were secretly moved to the United States. Their past record of working for the Nazis was covered up. U.S. authorities believed that rocket technology was more valuable than punishing the scientists for their role in the war.

1944 U.S. workers at IBM complete the Harvard Mark I calculator.

1944 Russian-born U.S. engineer Igor Sikorsky builds the VS-36A, which sets the design of the modern helicopter.

1944 U.S. physicist Robert Dicke makes a radiometer for detecting microwave radiation.

1944

1944 U.S. physical chemist Glenn Seaborg isolates the radioactive elements americium and curium.

1944 U.S. chemist Robert Woodward leads the synthesis of the antimalarial drug quinine.

1944 U.S. bacteriologist Oswald Avery shows that nearly all organisms have DNA as their hereditary material.

Nuclear Fission

In the early 20th century, physicists realized that bombarding atoms with subatomic particles could release huge amounts of energy in a process called nuclear fission.

→→ The best-known use of nuclear fission was in the creation of the atom bomb.

TIMELINE
1945–1947

KEY:

- Astronomy and Math
- Biology and Medicine
- Chemistry and Physics
- Engineering and Invention

1945

1946

1945 U.S. government scientists make and test an atom bomb.

1945 Soviet physicist Vladimir Veksler designs and builds a powerful particle accelerator, the synchrocyclotron.

1946 U.S. computer engineers build ENIAC (Electronic Numerical Integrator and Computer), a fully electronic computer.

1945 English crystallographer Dorothy Hodgkin uses X-ray crystallography to determine the structure of penicillin.

1945 Chinese–American biochemist Choh Hao Li isolates the human growth hormone somatotropin.

1946 U.S. chemist Willard Libby begins work on radiocarbon dating, a chemical way to date old organic material.

Danish scientist Niels Bohr explained the principles behind nuclear fission.

I n 1932, John Cockcroft and Ernest Walton experimented with high-energy protons in the particle accelerator at the Cavendish Laboratory in Cambridge, England. In Paris in 1934, Irène and Frédéric Joliot-Curie found that proton bombardment sometimes produced radioactive isotopes. Two years later, Enrico Fermi found neutrons were more effective than protons at smashing atoms.

Splitting the Atom

In 1939, Otto Hahn and Fritz Strassmann identified the products of uranium bombardment. Hahn and Strassmann had demonstrated that the uranium nuclei had broken apart. "Fission" had occurred.

The same year, Lise Meitner and her nephew Otto Frisch, working with Niels Bohr, explained this result. Hahn and Strassmann found that as well as a large amount of energy,

Timeline

1932 Cockcroft and Walton particle accelerator

1934 Joliot-Curies produce radioactive isotopes

1936 Fermi uses neutrons to smash atoms

1939 Hahn and Strassmann identify products of uranium fission

1942 First nuclear reactor

1945 First atom bomb tested

1951 Nuclear reactor built to generate electricity

Italian physicist Enrico Fermi designed the first working nuclear reactor, which became operational at Chicago University in 1942.

1946 English engineer Frederic Williams makes a computer memory using a cathode ray tube.

1947 Italian biologist Rita Levi-Montalcini finds nerve growth factor (NGF) in chick embryos.

1947 U.S. architect Buckminster Fuller invents geodesic dome construction for large buildings.

1947

1946 U.S. engineer Percy Spencer invents the microwave oven.

1947 U.S. airman Charles "Chuck" Yeager makes the first supersonic flight, in a Bell X-1 rocket-propelled airplane.

1947 U.S. inventor Edwin Land demonstrates the Polaroid camera.

Uranium Fission

Fission occurs when an atomic nucleus breaks in two with the release of two or three neutrons. It can be induced by firing neutrons or protons at a nucleus. Fission releases an amount of energy equal to the energy that bound the nucleus together. When a neutron strikes a 235U atom, the nucleus absorbs it, becoming 236U, which divides into two lighter nuclei with the release of neutrons. If the neutrons strike other 235U nuclei, they too undergo fission, setting up a chain reaction.

uranium fission released neutrons that may trigger fission in uranium nuclei, which create the possibility of a chain reaction.

Exploiting the Power of Fission

At the start of World War II, Bohr and John Wheeler published a paper describing the complete fission process. Meanwhile, Francis Perrin showed a certain "critical mass" of uranium is needed to sustain a chain

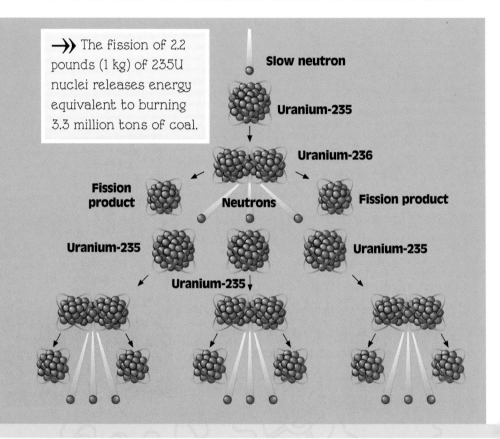

⟫ The fission of 2.2 pounds (1 kg) of 235U nuclei releases energy equivalent to burning 3.3 million tons of coal.

Slow neutron

Uranium-235

Uranium-236

Fission product

Neutrons

Fission product

Uranium-235

Uranium-235

Uranium-235

Uranium-235

TIMELINE
1948–1949

KEY:

- Astronomy and Math
- Biology and Medicine
- Chemistry and Physics
- Engineering and Invention

1948

1948 U.S. brothers Harold and Horace Babcock detect the sun's magnetic field.

1948 U.S. biochemists introduce the use of cortisone to treat rheumatoid arthritis.

1948 U.S. physicists propose a big bang theory for the origin of the universe.

1948 U.S. physicists Richard Feynman and Julian Schwinger independently formulate new versions of quantum electrodynamics.

1948 U.S. electrical engineer Peter Goldmark invents the long-playing phonograph record.

1948 U.S. musician Leo Fender and his colleagues market the first solid-body electric guitar.

reaction. Designed by Fermi, the first working reactor began operating in 1942, at the University of Chicago. In 1951, the Experimental Breeder Reactor in Idaho became the first reactor to generate electricity.

It became apparent that a sustained fission reaction could be used to create a bomb of immense power. Work to develop an atom bomb began in Britain and the United States. The two programs were merged in August 1942 to form the Manhattan Project. The first successful test of a bomb took place in New Mexico on July 16, 1945. Atomic bombs were dropped on the Japanese cities of Hiroshima and Nagasaki in August 1945. The Japanese surrendered shortly afterward.

↑ Scientists watch a controlled chain reaction in the "atomic pile" at the University of Chicago in 1942. Because of the radiation, no photographs could be taken, so the event was recorded by an artist.

1949 U.S. microbiologists culture the virus that causes poliomyelitis.

1949 U.S. chemists produce the radioactive element berkelium by bombarding americium with alpha particles.

1949 U.S. astronomer Frank Whipple suggest that comets are "dirty snowballs," consisting mainly of ice and rocky debris.

1949

1949 The first jet airliner, the de Havilland Comet, flies in England.

1949 English chemists use pulses of light in flash photolysis, for analyzing ultrafast chemical reactions.

1949 U.S. computer pioneers John Eckert and John Mauchly construct BINAC, a binary automatic computer.

Glossary

amplifier An electronic device that increases the strength of an input current or voltage.

antibiotic A chemical substance that can destroy or inhibit the growth of bacteria or other microorganisms.

atom The smallest unit into which matter can be divided and still retain its chemical identity.

bacillus A cylindrical-shaped bacterium.

bacteria (singular bacterium) Microscopic organisms that can cause disease.

cathode The negative electrode of a battery or similar device, through which an electric current passes.

cathode ray A stream of electrons emitted by a cathode when heated.

electron A negatively charged subatomic particle.

enzyme A large protein molecule that acts as a catalyst for the chemical reactions on which life depends.

neutron An uncharged subatomic particle in the atomic nucleus.

nuclear reactor A device for generating electricity by nuclear fission or nuclear fusion.

nucleus, atomic (plural nuclei) The positively charged dense region at the center of an atom, composed of protons and neutrons.

photon The basic particle of energy in which light and other forms of electromagnetic radiation are emitted.

proton A positively charged subatomic particle in the atomic nucleus.

radar An acronym for radio direction and ranging; a device that uses radio waves for detecting distant objects.

radioactivity The emission of particles or radiation by atomic nuclei.

subatomic particle Any particle that is smaller than an atom.

vaccine A preparation containing viruses or other microorganisms introduced (often by injection) into the body to stimulate the formation of antibodies to build up immunity against infectious disease.

virus A tiny parasitic organism that can only reproduce inside the cell of its host.

Further Reading

Books

Ballard, Carol. *From Cowpox to Antibiotics: Discovering Vaccines and Medicines.* Chicago: Heinemann Library, 2006.

Collier, James Lincoln. *The Automobile (Great Inventions).* New York: Benchmark Books, 2005.

Hansen, Ole Steen. *The Story of Flight.* New York: Crabtree Publishing Company, 2004.

Morton, Alan Q. *Splitting the Atom.* Milwaukee: World Almanac Library, 2005.

O'Shei, Tim. *Marconi and Tesla: Pioneers of Radio Communication.* Berkeley Heights, NJ: MyReportLinks.com Books, 2008.

Otfinski, Steve. *Television* (Great Inventions). New York: Benchmark Books, 2006.

Parker, Katie, and Denise Pangia. *Splitting the Atom.* New York: Marshall Cavendish Children's Books, 2009.

Parker, Lewis K. *Henry Ford and the Automobile Industry.* New York: PowerKids Press, 2003.

Rosinsky, Natalie Myra. *The Story of Pharmaceuticals: How They Changed the World.* Minneapolis, MN: Compass Point Books, 2010.

Sonneborn, Liz. *Guglielmo Marconi: Inventor of Wireless Technology.* New York: Children's Press, 2005.

Tocci, Salvatore. *Alexander Fleming: The Man Who Discovered Penicillin.* Berkeley Heights, NJ: Enslow Publishers, 2002.

Venezia, Mike. *The Wright Brothers: Inventors Whose Ideas Really Took Flight.* New York: Children's Press, 2010.

Web Sites

http://firstflight.open.ac.uk/
Site with interactive history of flight.

http://inventors.about.com/od/cstartinventions/a/Car_History.htm
About.com site on the history of the automobile, with links to inventors.

http://www.scienceclarified.com/Mu-Oi/Nuclear-Fission.html
Science Clarified pages about nuclear fission.

http://205.188.238.181/time/time100/scientist/profile/fleming.html
Time Magazine site proposing Alexander Fleming as one of the most notable people of the 20th century.

Index

airplane 14–17
amplitude modulation 8, **8**
antibiotics 30–33
aspirin 20, **20**, 21
assembly line 13
atom bomb 45
atoms 22–25
automobile 10–13

bacteria 31, 32
Baird, John Logie 26–28
BBC 28
Benz, Karl 12
    automobile **11**
Blériot, Louis **17**
Bohr, Neils **43**

cathode-ray tube 29, **29**
Cavendish Laboratory 23
Chadwick, James 24
Cockcroft, John 23, 25, 43

Daimler, Gottlieb 12–13
    autmobile **11**
Davy, Humphry 19
drugs, synthetic 18–21
Duryea, Charles 13

electromagnetism 7, 24

Farnsworth, Philo 29
Fermi, Enrico 43, **43**, 46
fission, nuclear 42–45
Fleming, Alexander 31, 32, 33

flight 14–17
Flyer **14**, 16, **16**
Ford, Henry 13

glider 15, **15**

Hertz, Heinrich 7
Hülsmeyer, Christian 35, **35**

iconoscope 28, **28**

Joliot-Curie, Irène and Frédéric 24, 43

Large Hadron Collider **24**
Lilienthal, Otto 15, **15**

magnetron 36, **36**, 37
Manhattan Project 45
Marconi, Guglielmo 7, 9, **9**
Maxwell, James Clerk 7
medicines 18–21
missiles 39, 40
Model T Ford **10**, **11**, 13, **13**

NASA 40
Nipkov disk 27, **27**
nuclear reactor 43, 45, **45**

Panhard and Levassor **11**, 13
particle accelerator 23, 25, **25**

Pasteur, Louis 31, 32
Pauli, Wolfgang 25
penicillin 30–33
proton 23

radar 34–37
radio 6–9
rockets 38–41
Rutherford, Ernest 23, **23**

salicylic acid 20, **20**, 21
space program 41, **41**
steam vehicles 11–12
subatomic particles 22–25

television 26–29

University of Chicago **43**, **45**
uranium 43, 44, **44**

V-2 **38**, 39, 40, **40**
Von Braun, Werner 38–41

Walton, Ernest 23, 25, 43
willow 20, **21**
World War II 33, **33**, 37, 38, 39, 40, **40**, 41, 44–45
Wright Brothers 14, 15, 16, 17

Zworykin, Vladimir 28, 29